D1469156

HOW TO COOK HOLIDAY ROASTS & BIRDS

An illustrated step-by-step guide to roast
turkey, goose, Cornish hens, ham,
prime rib, and leg of lamb.

THE COOK'S ILLUSTRATED LIBRARY

Illustrations by John Burgoyne

BOSTON COMMON PRESS
Brookline, Massachusetts

1998

Boston Common Press
17 Station Street
Brookline, Massachusetts 02146

ISBN 0-936184-28-0
Library of Congress Cataloging-in-Publication Data
The Editors of *Cook's Illustrated*

How to cook holiday roasts and birds: An illustrated step-by-step guide to roast turkey, goose, Cornish hens, ham, prime rib, and leg of lamb/The Editors of *Cook's Illustrated*
1st ed.

Includes 22 recipes and 33 illustrations
ISBN 0-936184-28-0 (hardback): $14.95
I. Cooking. I. Title
1998

Manufactured in the United States of America

Distributed by Boston Common Press, 17 Station Street, Brookline, MA 02146.

Cover and text design: Amy Klee
Recipe development: Melissa Hamilton
Series editor: Jack Bishop

CONTENTS

introduction

In 1955, our family built a small cabin on a 20-acre piece of side hill in Vermont bought from Junior Bentley's father, Charlie. It started as a summer and weekend retreat, but a few years later we purchased the old Lomberg farm and raised pigs and Black Angus with the help of a local couple who did the chores when we weren't there. Since the farm included good bottom land running down to the Green River, my mother named our enterprise Green River Farm, the brand name we used when selling our sausage to local restaurants. We called it "Whole Hog" sausage, since we used even the prime parts of the pig to make our links.

In those days, the meat had plenty of fat and the roasts were succulent. Today, however, America's obsession with health has resulted in such low-fat meat that preparing a simple roast is quite a challenge. In these pages, we explain how we have managed to maximize flavor, texture, and moisture through a variety of techniques, including brining and low-heat roasting. Because each cut of meat is different, we tailor our methods to the roast at hand, preferring higher temperatures, for example, for lamb, whereas a rib roast can be cooked at a modest 200 degrees.

We also turn our attention to poultry, testing how best to reduce the amount of fat under the skin of a goose while, at the same time, making the meat juicier and more succulent. We found that dipping the bird in boiling water, refrigerating, and then roasting works wonders. We also brine the Thanksgiving turkey before roasting, which ensures that the white meat will not dry out. This book is full of similar fresh ideas for roasting, ideas that have been carefully tested in the kitchens of *Cook's Illustrated*.

This volume is part of a series of how-to books that includes american layer cakes, cookie jar favorites, grilling, holiday desserts, ice cream, pasta sauces, pies, pizza, salad, simple fruit desserts, and stir-fries. New titles will soon be available. To order books, call us at (800) 611-0759. We also publish *Cook's Illustrated,* a bimonthly publication about American home cooking. For a free trial copy of *Cook's,* call (800) 526-8442.

Christopher P. Kimball
Publisher and Editor
Cook's Illustrated

chapter one

ROASTING BASICS

LTHOUGH ROASTS COME FROM A VARIETY OF animals, they are all cooked in the oven, often in a similar fashion. Many of the issues are the same when roasting turkey or goose, prime rib or leg of lamb. What's the best oven temperature? Does the roast need to be turned? Is a rack necessary?

There are two basic styles of roasting. What might be termed "conventional roasting" starts with a moderate oven—350 or 375 degrees are standard temperatures. The roast is placed in the oven and then cooked at that initial oven temperature until the internal temperature of the meat reaches the desired number. Although this method is easy, it does not take full advantage of the oven's capabilities.

Other roasting methods manipulate the temperature, sometimes using a combination of higher and/or lower temperatures. High-heat roasting (temperatures of 400 degrees and higher) promotes exterior browning, which builds flavor, crisps any skin, and makes a roast more attractive. But high-heat roasting can cause uneven cooking, with the temperature of the exterior layers of meat racing ahead of the temperature in the center of the roast.

In general, high heat is better for small roasts and birds (like Cornish hens) that need to brown thoroughly by the time the meat is cooked through. High heat can also be used at the beginning of the cooking time to brown a roast or at the end of the cooking time to crisp the skin on a bird.

Slow roasting, or low-heat roasting, relies on temperatures of 325 degrees or lower to cook gently and evenly. Lower oven temperatures allow sufficient time for the even conduction of heat from the outer layers of a roast to the center. The main problem with slow-roasting is that the exterior will remain quite pale, even after hours in the oven. Many slow-roasting recipes either begin by searing the meat (prime rib) or end by raising the oven temperature (goose).

EQUIPMENT FOR ROASTING

Roasting requires a few pieces of equipment. In addition to

the list below, you will need a carving board and some knives.

▓ INSTANT-READ THERMOMETER We recommend an instant-read thermometer over traditional meat thermometers that are inserted into the roast before it goes into the oven. An instant-read thermometer can be inserted into almost any food—everything from a roast to a custard for ice cream—and will display the internal temperature within seconds. Unlike traditional meat thermometers, instant-read thermometers are not designed to be left in the oven. Prolonged exposure of the whole unit to heat will destroy the measuring mechanism.

There are two types of instant-read thermometers on the market—dial face and digital. Though pocket-size dial face thermometers are less expensive than digitals, they are less precise, and most read temperatures in a narrower range. Our favorite thermometer registers temperatures from below zero to 500 degrees.

Another important difference between digital and dial thermometers is the location of the temperature sensor. On dial face thermometers, the sensors are roughly 1½ inches from the tip of the stem. The sensors on digital thermometers are usually located at the very tip of the stem. The former position means that the stem must be stuck deep into the meat or other food. A digital thermometer will deliver a more accurate reading in thin cutlets or shallow liquids.

There is one last factor to consider when buying an instant-read thermometer. In our testing of nine models, we found that some models responded in just 10 seconds, while others took as long as 30 seconds to record the correct temperature. There is no point keeping the oven door open longer than is necessary, so choose a fast-responding model such as the Owen Instruments Thermapen or Taylor Digital Pocket.

▦ ROASTING PAN Roasting pans can cost $2 or $200, or even more once you start talking about copper. Most roasting pans are made of aluminum because it heats quickly. Some pans are lined with stainless steel, which is easier to clean than aluminum. We find that material is less important than size, depth, and weight.

You want a roasting pan that is large enough to hold a leg of lamb or country ham. A 13- by 9-inch baking pan is fine for a chicken, but you will need something considerably larger for most roasts. A size of 15 by 12 inches will work fine for most recipes in this book. (You will need a roasting or jelly roll pan that measures 19-inches long and 13-inches across to cook six Cornish hens at one time.)

In addition to size, you want a roasting pan that is deep

enough to keep fat from splattering onto the walls of the oven. Since many roasts are cooked on racks, a shallow pan may prove problematic. On the other hand, a really deep pan will discourage browning. We find that a depth of 2½ inches is ideal.

We also prefer roasting pans with handles, which make it easy to lift them in and out of the oven. Lastly, you should consider buying a roasting pan with a heavy bottom. Some recipes end by placing the empty pan on top of the stove for deglazing. A thin pan may buckle or scorch, but a heavy-duty roasting pan with a thick bottom won't.

We know that many cooks rely on disposable aluminum pans for holiday roasts and birds. They are large and cheap and there is no cleanup. The downside is that these pans are flimsy and can fall apart. If you insist on using them, fit two pans together to support heavy roasts and birds. Also, try to buy disposable pans with handles and make sure to support the bottom of the filled pan when lifting it.

ROASTING RACK A rack keeps a roast above pan juices and grease, which helps prevent the exterior from cooking up soft or fatty. A rack also allows air to circulate underneath so the bottom of a roast can brown without burning or overcooking, which sometimes happens when a roast rests directly on a hot pan.

There are several types of roasting racks, each with a different use. A U-shaped basket rack cradles a chicken perfectly. In our test, we found that the perforated nonstick finish conducts heat better than other racks so that skin browns especially well. Basket racks are solid and stable, but too small to accommodate turkeys or geese. For these larger birds, a nonadjustable V-rack is recommended. Unlike adjustable V-racks, the nonadjustable version is made from thick metal bars, not flimsy wires. We found that this kind of rack stays put in the pan and doesn't bend when holding heavy birds.

Basket and V-racks keep birds well elevated from the roasting pan so that the skin on the underside browns well. In our tests, we found that a vertical rack doesn't lift the chicken far enough off the pan to brown the skin on the bottom end of the bird. A vertical rack also splatters fat all over the oven.

For other recipes, you simply need to keep the meat out of the rendered fat and juices. A flat rack is fine for prime rib, ham, or leg of lamb. Look for special roasting racks that are small enough to fit in most pans.

chapter two

ROAST TURKEY

I S IT POSSIBLE TO ROAST A TURKEY PERFECTLY? Usually juicy breast meat comes with a price—shocking pink legs and thighs. You have some leeway with the dark meat, which is almost impossible to dry out during normal roasting times. The problem is that the breast, which is exposed to direct heat and finishes cooking at a lower temperature, becomes parched while the legs and thighs take their time creeping to doneness. Nearly every roasting method in existence tries to compensate for this; few succeed.

We tested dozens of different methods for roasting a turkey, from traditional to idiosyncratic. Our goals were to end up with an attractive bird, to determine the ideal internal temperature, and to find a method that would finish both white and dark meat simultaneously.

Our first roasting experiments used the method most frequently promoted by the National Turkey Federation, the United States Department of Agriculture, and legions of cookbook authors and recipe writers. This method features a moderately low roasting temperature of 325 degrees, a breast-up bird, and an open pan. We tried this method twice, basting one turkey and leaving the other alone. The basted turkey acquired a beautifully tanned skin, while the unbasted bird remained quite pale. Both were cooked to 170 degrees in the leg/thigh. Despite the fact that this was 10 degrees lower than recommended by the USDA and most producers, the breasts still registered a throat-catchingly dry 180 degrees.

We quickly determined that almost all turkeys roasted in the traditional breast-up manner produced breast meat that was 10 degrees ahead of the leg/thigh meat (tenting the breast with heavy-duty foil was the exception; read on). Because white meat is ideal at 160 degrees, and dark thigh meat just loses its last shades of pink at about 170 degrees, you might conclude, as we did, that roasting turkeys with their breasts up is a losing proposition.

We also discovered that stuffing a bird makes overcooked meat more likely. Because it slows interior cooking (our tests showed a nearly 30-degree difference in internal temperature after an hour in the oven), stuffing means longer oven times, which can translate to bone-dry surface meat. We eventually developed a method for roasting a stuffed turkey (*see* page 28), but if the turkey is your priority, we recommend cooking the dressing separately.

Of all the breast-up methods, tenting the bird's breast and upper legs with foil, as suggested by numerous authors, worked the best. The foil deflects some of the oven's heat, reducing the ultimate temperature differential between white and dark meat from 10 to 6 degrees. The bird is roasted at a consistent 325-degree temperature, and during the last 45 minutes of roasting the foil is removed, allowing enough time for lovely browning. If you're partial to open-pan roasting and don't care to follow the technique we developed, try the foil shield; it certainly ran second in our tests.

Amidst all these failures and near-successes, some real winners did emerge. Early on, we became fans of brining turkey in a salt water bath before roasting. When we first removed the brined turkey from the refrigerator, we found a beautiful, milky-white bird. When roasted, the texture of the breast was different from that of the other birds we had cooked; the meat was firm and juicy at the same time. And the turkey tasted fully seasoned; others had required a bite of skin with the meat to achieve the same effect. We experimented with the brining time, and found that eight to 12 hours in the refrigerator produces a pleasantly seasoned turkey without overly salty pan juices. Brining was our first real breakthrough; we now believe it to be essential in achieving perfect taste and texture. But we had yet to discover the way to roast.

Our most successful attempt at achieving equal temperatures in leg and breast came when we followed James Beard's technique of turning the turkey as it roasts. In this method, the bird begins breast side down on a V-rack, then spends equal time on each of its sides before being turned breast side up. The V-rack is important not just to hold the turkey in place, but also to elevate the turkey, affording it some protection from the heat of the roasting pan. This combination of rack and technique produced a turkey with a breast temperature that ran only a few degrees behind the leg temperature.

Because we were using smaller turkeys than Beard had used, we had to fine-tune his method. Large turkeys spend enough time in the oven to brown at 350 degrees; our turkeys were in the 12-pound range and were cooking in as little as two hours, yielding quite pale skin. Clearly, we needed higher heat.

Reviewing our notes, we noticed that the basted birds

were usually the evenly browned, beautiful ones. So we turned up the heat to 400 degrees, basted faithfully, and got what we wanted. In an effort to streamline, we tried to skip the leg-up turns, roasting only breast side down, then breast side up. But in order for the turkey to brown all over, these two extra turns were necessary. Brining, turning, and basting are work, yes, but the combination produces the best turkey we've ever had.

During our first few tests, we discovered that filling the cavity with aromatic herbs and vegetables made for a subtle but perceptible difference in flavor. This was especially noticeable in the inner meat of the leg and thigh; turkeys with hollow cavities, by contrast, tasted bland. Roasted alongside the turkey, the same combination of carrot, celery, onion, and thyme also did wonders for the pan juices.

INTERNAL TEMPERATURE: HOW MUCH IS ENOUGH?

Industry standards developed by the United States Department of Agriculture and the National Turkey Federation call for whole birds to be cooked to an internal thigh temperature of 180 to 185 degrees. The breast temperature, according to these standards, should be 170 degrees. However, our kitchen tests showed that no meat is at its best at a temperature of 180 or 185 degrees. And breast meat really tastes best closer to 160 to 165 degrees.

While the USDA might have us believe that the only safe turkey is a dry turkey, this just isn't true. The two main bacterial problems in turkey are salmonella and Campylobacter jejuni. According to USDA standards, salmonella in meat is killed at 160 degrees. Turkey is no different. So why the higher safety standard of 180 degrees?

Part of the problem is that stuffing must reach an internal temperature of 165 degrees to be considered safe. (Carbohydrates such as bread provide a better medium for bacterial growth than do proteins such as meat; hence the extra safety margin of 5 degrees). The USDA also worries that most cooks don't own an accurate thermometer.

The final word on poultry safety is this: As long as the temperature on an accurate instant-read thermometer reaches 160 degrees when inserted in several places, all unstuffed meat (including turkey) should be bacteria-free. Dark meat is undercooked at this stage and tastes better at 170 or 175 degrees. With our turning method, the breast will reach about 165 degrees when the leg is done.

A temperature of 165 degrees also guarantees that stuffed turkeys are safe. But bacteria in meat cooked to 180 or 185 degrees is long gone—as is moistness and flavor.

Best Roast Turkey

➤ NOTE: *We prefer to roast small turkeys, no more than 14 pounds gross weight, because they cook more evenly than large birds. (If you must cook a large bird, see the variation on page 22.) If you prefer, double the amount of salt in the brine and brine for just four hours. This hurry-up brine works with large turkeys and turkeys destined to be stuffed as well. Serves 10 to 12.*

2	cups kosher salt or 1 cup table salt
1	turkey (12 to 14 pounds gross weight), rinsed thoroughly; giblets, neck, and tailpiece removed and reserved to make gravy (*see* page 26)
3	medium onions, chopped coarse
1½	medium carrots, chopped coarse
1½	celery stalks, chopped coarse
6	thyme sprigs
3	tablespoons unsalted butter, melted

❚❚ INSTRUCTIONS:

1. Dissolve salt in 2 gallons of cold water in large stockpot or clean bucket. Add turkey and refrigerate or set in very cool (40 degrees or less) spot for 12 hours.

2. Remove turkey from salt water and rinse both cavities and skin under cool running water for several minutes until all traces of salt are gone. Pat dry inside and out with paper towels. Adjust oven rack to lowest position and heat oven to 400 degrees. Toss one-third of onion, carrot, celery, and thyme with 1 tablespoon of melted butter and place this mixture in body cavity. Bring turkey legs together and perform a simple truss (*see* figures 1–3).

3. Scatter remaining vegetables and thyme over a shallow roasting pan. Pour 1 cup water over vegetables. Set V-rack in pan. Brush entire breast side of turkey with half of remaining butter, then place turkey, breast side down, on V-rack. Brush entire backside of turkey with remaining butter.

4. Roast for 45 minutes. Remove pan from oven (close oven door); baste. With wad of paper toweling in each hand, turn turkey, leg/thigh side up. If liquid in pan has totally evaporated, add additional ½ cup water. Return turkey to oven and roast for 15 minutes. Remove turkey from oven again, baste, and again use paper toweling to turn other leg/thigh side up; roast for another 15 minutes. Remove turkey from oven for final time, baste, and turn it breast side up; roast until breast registers about 165 degrees and thigh registers 170 to 175 degrees on an instant-read thermometer, 30 to 45 minutes (*see* figures 4 and 5). Remove turkey from pan and let rest until ready to carve. Serve with gravy.

▪▪ VARIATION:

Large Roast Turkey

Smaller turkeys cook faster and are generally more tender, but sometimes you need a bigger bird for a large holiday crowd. By tinkering with our original recipe, we were able to produce a beautiful large turkey without sacrificing juiciness and flavor. When roasting a large turkey, it's not necessary to roast bird on each side. Serves 18 to 20.

Follow recipe for Best Roast Turkey, roasting 18- to 20-pound turkey breast side down in 250-degree oven for 3 hours, basting every hour. Then turn breast side up and roast another hour, basting once or twice. Increase oven temperature to 400 degrees and roast until done, about 1 hour longer.

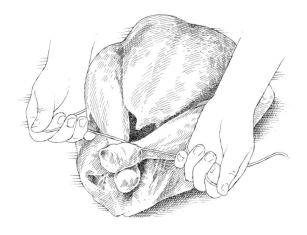

Figure 1.
Using the center of a 5-foot length of cooking twine, tie the legs
together at the ankles.

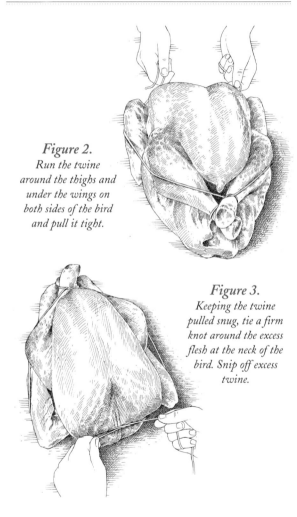

Figure 2.
Run the twine around the thighs and under the wings on both sides of the bird and pull it tight.

Figure 3.
Keeping the twine pulled snug, tie a firm knot around the excess flesh at the neck of the bird. Snip off excess twine.

Figure 4.
When using an instant-read thermometer, make sure that you measure the temperature of the thickest part of the thigh.

Figure 5.
This cutaway drawing shows the actual point to which the tip of the thermometer should penetrate.

Giblet Pan Gravy

➤ **NOTE:** *The gravy is best made over several hours. Complete step 1 while the turkey is brining. Continue with step 2 once the bird is in the oven. Start step 3 once the bird has been removed from the oven and is resting on a carving board.*

1	tablespoon vegetable oil
	Reserved turkey giblets, neck, and tailpiece
1	onion, unpeeled and chopped
1½	quarts turkey or chicken stock or 1 quart low-sodium canned chicken broth plus
2	cups water
2	thyme branches
8	parsley stems
3	tablespoons unsalted butter
¼	cup flour
1	cup dry white wine
	Salt and ground black pepper

INSTRUCTIONS:

1. Heat oil in soup kettle; add giblets, neck, and tail, then sauté until golden and fragrant, about 5 minutes. Add onion; continue to sauté until softened, 3 to 4 minutes longer. Reduce heat to low; cover and cook until turkey and onion release their juices, about 20 minutes. Add stock and herbs, bring to boil, then adjust heat to low. Simmer, skimming any scum that may rise to surface, until broth is rich and flavorful, about 30 minutes longer. Strain broth (you should have about 5 cups) and reserve neck, heart, and gizzard. When cool enough to handle, shred neck meat, remove gristle from gizzard, then dice reserved heart and gizzard. Refrigerate giblets and broth until ready to use.

2. While turkey is roasting, return reserved turkey broth to simmer. Heat butter in large heavy-bottomed saucepan over medium-low heat. Vigorously whisk in flour. Cook slowly, stirring constantly, until nutty brown and fragrant, 10 to 15 minutes. Vigorously whisk all but 1 cup of hot broth into roux. Bring to boil, then continue to simmer until gravy is lightly thickened and very flavorful, about 30 minutes longer. Set aside until turkey is done.

3. When turkey has been transferred to carving board to rest, spoon out and discard as much fat as possible from roasting pan, leaving caramelized herbs and vegetables. Place roasting pan over two burners at medium-high heat. Return gravy to simmer. Add wine to roasting pan of caramelized vegetables, scraping up any browned bits with wooden spoon and boiling until reduced by half, about 5 minutes. Add remaining 1 cup broth, then strain pan juices into gravy, pressing as much juice as possible out of vegetables. Stir giblets into gravy; return to a boil. Adjust seasonings, adding salt and pepper to taste. Serve with turkey.

Roast Stuffed Turkey

➤ **NOTE:** *For some cooks, the stuffing is the best part of the holiday meal, and for best flavor they want to cook at least some of the stuffing in the bird. This causes all kinds of cooking problems since the stuffing can be slow to heat up. The stuffing enthusiasts in our test kitchen developed a method that gets the stuffing hot enough to kill any bacteria without causing the delicate breast meat to dry out.*

At the outset, we limited our turkey to a maximum of 15 pounds because it is just too difficult to stuff and roast larger birds safely. From initial tests, we saw that the stuffing generally lagged at least 10 degrees behind the breast and leg. Since the stuffing must reach a temperature of 165 degrees according to USDA standards, our breast meat was at a bone-dry 175 degrees in these early experiments.

Clearly, we were going to have to heat the stuffing before putting it into the turkey. When we heated stuffing to 120 degrees in a microwave and then roasted the bird at a constant 325 degrees, we cut 45 minutes off the roasting time we'd needed with cold stuffing. The breast was still overcooked, but this method was promising. In the end, we settled on a combination of high and low heat.

We also determined that, regardless of temperature, roasting the bird breast down for only one hour was not sufficient. The breast needed to be shielded for most of the cooking time. We also abandoned roasting leg side up because the turns were too awkward with a stuffed bird.

A 12- to 15-pound turkey will accommodate approximately half of the stuffing. Bake the remainder in a casserole dish while the bird rests before carving. Make the gravy recipe on page 26. Serves 10 to 12.

2 cups kosher or 1 cup table salt

1 turkey (12 to 15 pounds gross weight) rinsed thoroughly; giblets, neck, and tailpiece removed and reserved to make gravy (*see* page 26)

2 medium onions, chopped coarse

1 medium carrot, chopped coarse

1 celery stalk, chopped coarse

4 thyme sprigs

12 cups prepared stuffing (*see* pages 33–37)

3 tablespoons unsalted butter, plus extra to grease casserole dish and foil

¼ cup turkey or chicken stock or low-sodium canned chicken broth

INSTRUCTIONS:

1. Dissolve salt in 2 gallons of cold water in large stock pot or clean bucket. Add turkey and refrigerate or set in very cool (40 degrees or less) spot for 12 hours.

2. Remove turkey from salt water and rinse skin and both cavities under cool water for several minutes until all traces of salt are gone. Pat dry inside and out with paper towels; set aside. Adjust oven rack to the lowest position and heat the oven to 400 degrees. Scatter onions, carrot, celery, and thyme over shallow roasting pan. Pour 1 cup water over vegetables. Set V-rack in pan.

3. Place half of stuffing in buttered medium casserole dish, dot surface with 1 tablespoon butter, cover with buttered foil, and refrigerate until ready to use. Microwave remaining stuffing on full power, stirring two or three times, until very hot (120 to 130 degrees), 6 to 8 minutes (if you can handle stuffing with hands, it is not hot enough). Spoon 4 to 5 cups of stuffing into the turkey cavity until very loosely packed (*see* figure 6). Secure skin flap over the cavity opening with turkey lacers or skewers (*see* figures 7 and 8). Melt remaining 2 tablespoons butter. Tuck wings behind back, brush entire breast side with half of melted butter, then place turkey breast side down on V-rack. Fill neck cavity with remaining heated stuffing and secure skin flap over opening as above (*see* figure 9). Brush back with remaining butter.

4. Roast 1 hour, then reduce temperature to 250 degrees and roast 2 hours longer, adding additional water if pan becomes dry. Remove pan from oven (close oven door) and with wad of paper toweling in each hand, turn breast side up and baste (temperature of breast should be 145 to 150 degrees). Increase oven temperature to 400 degrees; continue roasting until breast registers about 165 degrees, thigh registers 170 to 175 degrees, and stuffing registers 165 degrees on instant-read thermometer, 1 to 1½ hours longer. Remove turkey from oven and let rest until ready to carve.

5. Add ¼ cup stock to dish of reserved stuffing, replace foil, and bake until hot throughout, about 20 minutes. Remove foil; continue to bake until stuffing forms golden brown crust, about 15 minutes longer.

6. Carve turkey; serve with stuffing and gravy.

Figure 6.
Use a measuring cup to place the preheated stuffing into the
cavity of the bird. Remember, it's imperative that the
stuffing is heated before placing it in the bird.

Figure 7.
To keep the stuffing in the cavity use metal skewers (or cut bamboo skewers) and thread them through the skin on both sides of the cavity.

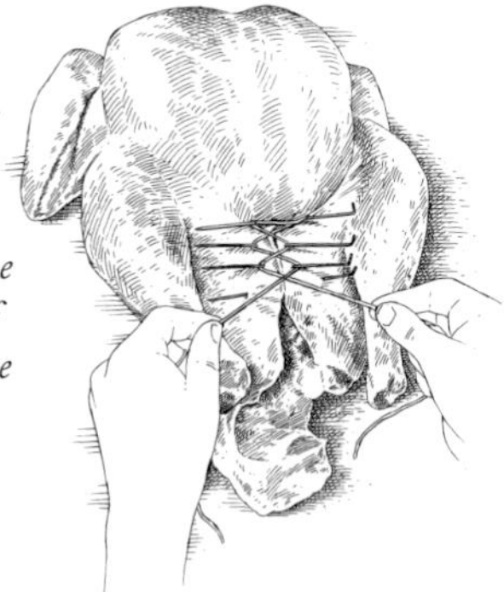

Figure 8.
Use a 2-foot piece of kitchen twine to close up the cavity, as if you were lacing up boots. Center the twine on the top skewer and then simply cross the twine as you wrap each end of the string around and under the skewers. Loosely tie the legs together with another short piece of kitchen twine.

Figure 9.
Flip the bird over onto its breast. Stuff the neck cavity loosely with approximately one cup of stuffing. Pull the skin flap over and use a skewer to pin the flap to the turkey.

3 2

ALL ABOUT BREAD STUFFINGS

In our tests, we found that dry bread cubes are essential when making stuffing because they do a better job of absorbing seasonings and other flavors than fresh cubes. To dry bread, cut a fresh loaf of French or other white bread into ½-inch slices, place the slices in a single layer on cookie sheets or cooling racks, and allow the slices to sit out overnight. The next day, cut the slices into ½-inch cubes and allow them to dry in a single layer for an additional night.

If you are in a hurry, place ½-inch slices of bread in a 225-degree oven for 30 to 40 minutes, or until dried but not browned. Remove the bread from the oven and cut into ½-inch cubes. You will need a one-pound loaf of bread to obtain the 12 cups of bread cubes necessary for the following recipes.

All these stuffings can be covered and refrigerated for one day. Turn the mixture into a 13-by-9-inch or comparably-sized microwave-safe pan and reheat in a 325 degree-oven or microwave until the stuffing is warmed through before packing it into a bird.

Place any stuffing that won't fit in the bird in a greased 8-inch square baking dish. Drizzle a few tablespoons of melted butter over the stuffing and cover the pan with foil. Bake in a 400-degree oven for about 25 minutes, remove the foil, and bake an additional 15 minutes. All of these bread stuffing recipes make about 12 cups.

Bread Stuffing with Sausage, Pecans, and Dried Apricots

➤ **NOTE:** *High-quality sausage is the key to this recipe. Toast the pecans in a 350-degree oven until fragrant, 6 to 8 minutes.*

1	pound sweet Italian sausage, removed from casings and crumbled
6	tablespoons unsalted butter
1	large onion, chopped (about 1½ cups)
4	medium celery stalks, chopped (about 1½ cups)
½	teaspoon each dried sage, dried thyme, dried marjoram
½	teaspoon ground black pepper
½	cup fresh parsley leaves, chopped fine
2	cups pecans, toasted and roughly chopped
1	cup dried apricots, sliced thin
1	teaspoon salt
12	cups dried French or other white bread cubes (*see* page 33)
1	cup chicken stock or low-sodium canned chicken broth
3	large eggs, lightly beaten

::INSTRUCTIONS:

1. Cook sausage in large skillet over medium heat until browned, about 10 minutes. Transfer sausage to large bowl with slotted spoon. Discard fat and in same pan melt butter.

2. Add onion and celery and cook, stirring occasionally, over medium heat until soft and translucent, 6 to 7 minutes. Add dried herbs and pepper and cook for another minute. Transfer contents of pan to bowl with sausage. Add parsley, pecans, apricots, and salt and mix to combine. Add bread cubes to bowl.

3. Whisk stock and eggs together in small bowl. Pour mixture over bread cubes. Gently toss to evenly distribute ingredients.

Bread Stuffing with Bacon, Apples, Sage, and Caramelized Onions

➤ NOTE: *For the best flavor, make sure to cook the onions until they are a deep golden brown color.*

1	pound bacon, cut crosswise into ¼ -inch strips
6	medium onions, sliced thin (about 7 cups)
1	teaspoon salt
2	Granny Smith apples, peeled, cored, and cut into ½ -inch cubes (about 2 cups)
½	teaspoon ground black pepper
½	cup fresh parsley leaves, chopped fine
3	tablespoons fresh sage leaves, cut into thin strips
½	cups dried French or other white bread cubes (*see* page 33)
1	cup chicken stock or low-sodium canned chicken broth
3	large eggs, lightly beaten

∷ INSTRUCTIONS:

1. Cook bacon in large skillet or Dutch oven over medium heat until crisp and browned, about 12 minutes. Remove bacon from pan with slotted spoon and drain on paper towels. Discard all but 3 tablespoons of rendered bacon fat.

2. Increase heat to medium-high and add onions and ¼ teaspoon of salt. Cook onions until golden in color, making sure to stir occasionally and scrape sides and bottom of pan, about 20 minutes. Reduce heat to medium and continue to cook, stirring more often to prevent burning, until onions are deep golden brown, another 5 minutes. Add apples and continue to cook another 5 minutes. Transfer contents of pan to large bowl.

3. Add remaining ¾ teaspoon salt, pepper, parsley, and sage to bowl and mix to combine. Add bread cubes.

4. Whisk stock and eggs together in small bowl. Pour mixture over bread cubes. Gently toss to evenly distribute ingredients.

chapter three

ROAST GOOSE

GOOSE MEAT IS SURPRISINGLY FIRM, ALMOST chewy to the bite, yet it is also moist and not at all tough or stringy. Both the breast and legs are dark, in the manner of duck, but unlike duck, goose has no gamy or tallowy undertones. Actually, the first impression of many people is that goose tastes a lot like roast beef.

Goose, however, does have a problem. Although the meat itself is not fatty, a thick layer of fat lies just below the skin. As a consequence, the skin, which looks so tempting, often turns out to be too soft and greasy to eat. To make a good roast goose, it is imperative to rid the bird of this fat.

38

Most cookbooks and chefs suggest periodic basting with chicken stock or wine to dissolve the fat and promote a handsome brown color. But this method does not work. A considerable amount of subcutaneous fat always remains, and worse, the basting seriously softens goose skin, which should be crackling crisp.

Among all the goose-cooking methods we had read about, we were most intrigued by the steam-roasting and closed-cover techniques recommended by various authorities. Since the best way to render fat is to simmer it in water, steaming sounded like a promising procedure.

So we set a goose on a rack over an inch of water and steamed it on top of the stove in a covered roaster for about an hour. Then we poured the water out of the pan and put the goose into a 325-degree oven, covered. After one hour we checked on the goose, and seeing that the skin was very flabby and not in the least bit brown, we removed the cover of the pan and turned the heat up to 350 degrees. Alas, an hour later the skin was still soft and only a little browner. Even though the goose tested done at this point, we let it stay in the oven for another 30 minutes, but the skin did not improve.

Tasting the goose, we realized that there was yet another problem; steaming had perhaps made the meat a tad juicier, but it had also made the texture a little rubbery and imparted a boiled, stewish flavor. The goose no longer tasted the way we thought goose should. So we abandoned steaming.

Since liquid basting and steaming had both proved unsuccessful, we thought it was time to try a simple dry roast. Some of the geese that we had bought came with instructions to roast at 500 degrees for 30 minutes and then to turn the oven down to 300 degrees and roast several hours longer. We stuffed the goose, dried and pricked the skin, and popped it into the scorching oven. As we should have guessed, within 15 minutes the goose had begun to drip, and the kitchen had filled with smoke. We quickly turned the oven thermostat down to 300 degrees and let the bird roast until it tested done, about three hours. Then we increased the oven temperature to 400 degrees, transferred the goose to a large jelly-roll pan, and returned it to the oven for about 15 minutes to brown and crisp the skin. The results surprised us. This method, the simplest of all, yielded a beautifully brown, crisp-skinned bird, with moist meat and surprisingly little unmelted fat.

Dry, open roasting looked like the way to proceed, but we wondered if the technique could be further improved. We thought about adapting a classic technique often used with duck. The duck is immersed in boiling water for one minute and then allowed to dry, uncovered, in the refrigerator for 24 hours. The boiling and drying were supposed to tighten the skin, so that during roasting, the fat would be squeezed out.

We tried this method with a goose and loved the results. The skin was papery-crisp and defatted to the point where it could be eaten with pleasure—and without guilt.

The breast and leg meat of a goose are not as dissimilar as the breast and leg meat of a chicken, turkey, or duck. Thus, while most birds require special roasting procedures—such as trussing or basting—to keep the breast at a lower temperature than the legs and to prevent it from drying out, goose can be put in the oven and left alone except for turning it over at the halfway mark to ensure even crisping of the skin.

Unlike these other birds, the doneness of goose cannot be judged solely by the internal temperature of the meat. The length of the cooking time is also an important factor. Goose generally reaches an internal temperature of 170 degrees in the thigh cavity (the usual indicator of "well done") after less than two hours of roasting. Yet the meat turns out to be tough, especially around the thighs, if the bird is removed from the oven at this point. At least 45 minutes of additional roasting are required to make the meat tender. Since goose has so much fat, there is little chance of the meat drying out. The most reliable indicator of doneness is the feel of the drumsticks. When the skin has puffed and the meat inside feels soft and almost shredded when pressed—like well-done stew meat—the rest of the bird should be just right.

Roast Goose

➤ NOTE: *We used both fresh and frozen geese in testing and found no difference in the final result. This is fortunate, as most geese come to the market frozen. Serves 8 to 10.*

1   whole goose (10 to 12 pounds gross weight), neck, giblets, wing tips, and excess fat removed, rinsed, patted dry, and reserved to make stuffing and stock (*see* page 47); wishbone removed and skin pricked all over (*see* figures 10–13)

8   cups Stuffing with Bacon, Apples, Sage, and Caramelized Onions (*see* page 36), warmed Salt and ground black pepper

1   recipe Red Wine Gravy (*see* page 48)

∷ INSTRUCTIONS:

1. Fill large stock pot two-thirds of way with water and bring to rolling boil. Submerge goose in boiling water (*see* figure 14). Drain goose and dry thoroughly, inside and out, with paper towels. Set goose, breast side up, on flat rack in roasting pan and refrigerate, uncovered, for 24 to 48 hours.

2. Adjust oven rack to low-center position and heat to 325 degrees. Stuff and truss goose (*see* figures 15 and 16). Season goose skin liberally with salt and pepper.

3. Place goose, breast down, on heavy-duty V-rack set over roasting pan; roast for 1½ hours. Remove goose from oven and bail out most of fat from roasting pan, being careful not to disturb browned bits at bottom of pan. Turn goose breast up, and return to oven to roast until flesh of drumsticks feels soft and broken up (like well-done stew meat) and skin has puffed up around breast bone and tops of thighs, 1¼ to 1½ hours longer. Increase oven temperature to 400 degrees; transfer goose, still on its rack, to large jelly-roll pan. Return to oven to further brown and fully crisp skin, about 15 minutes longer. Let stand, uncovered, about 30 minutes before carving.

4. Remove trussing, and spoon stuffing into serving bowl. Carve goose; serve with stuffing and gravy.

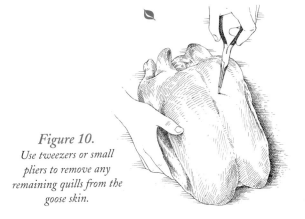

Figure 10.
Use tweezers or small
pliers to remove any
remaining quills from the
goose skin.

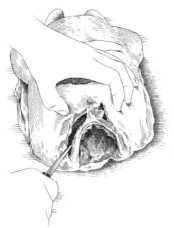

Figure 11.
Pull back the skin at the neck end and locate the wishbone. Scrape along the outside of the wishbone with a paring knife until the bone is exposed; then cut the bone free of the flesh.

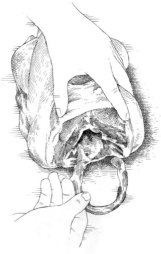

Figure 12.
Pull down on the wishbone, freeing it from the carcass; add the bone to the stock pot.

44

Figure 13.

With a trussing needle or thin skewer, prick the goose skin all over, especially around the breast and thighs, holding the needle nearly parallel to the bird to avoid pricking the meat. Pricking the skin helps render the fat during cooking.

Figure 14.

Using rubber gloves to protect your hands from possible splashes of boiling water, lower the goose, neck end down, into the water, submerging as much of the goose as possible until "goose bumps" appear, about 1 minute. Repeat this process, submerging the goose tail end down.

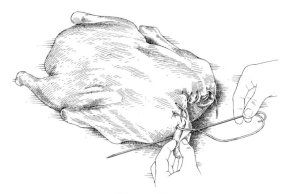

Figure 15.
Pack a small handful of stuffing into the neck cavity; sew the
opening shut with a trussing needle and heavy white twine.

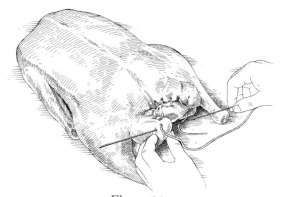

Figure 16.
Pack the remaining stuffing in the body cavity, pressing it in
firmly with your hands or a large spoon; sew the body vent shut.

Brown Goose Stock

➤ **NOTE:** *The goose stock can be cooled to room temperature and refrigerated in the saucepan up to 3 days. Makes about 1½ cups.*

3	tablespoons goose fat, patted dry and chopped
	Reserved goose neck and wing tips, cut into 1-inch pieces; heart and gizzard left whole
1	medium onion, chopped
1	medium carrot, peeled and chopped
1	medium celery stalk, chopped
2	teaspoons sugar
2	cups full-bodied red wine
½	cup chicken stock or low-sodium canned chicken broth
6	large parsley stems
1	large bay leaf
1	teaspoon black peppercorns
½	teaspoon dried thyme

⠿ INSTRUCTIONS:

1. Heat fat over medium heat in large saucepan until it melts, leaving small browned bits. Increase heat to medium-high; heat fat until it just begins to smoke. Add goose pieces; sauté, stirring until meat turns mahogany, about 10 minutes.

2. Add onion, carrot, and celery; sauté, stirring frequently, until vegetables brown around edges, about 10 minutes longer. Stir in sugar; continue to cook, stirring continuously, until it caramelizes and begins to smoke. Pour in wine, scraping pan bottom with wooden spoon to dissolve browned bits.

3. Add chicken stock, parsley, bay leaf, peppercorns, and thyme. Bring to simmer, lower heat so liquid barely bubbles. Simmer, partially covered, until stock is dark and rich, about 2 hours, adding water if solids become exposed.

❧

Red Wine Giblet Gravy

➤ **NOTE:** *This simple gravy starts with the Brown Goose Stock and then uses sherry to deglaze the roasting pan with the browned bits from the goose. Make the stock while the goose is in the oven and then start this gravy once the goose has been transferred to a carving board to rest. Makes about 2 cups.*

1	recipe Brown Goose Stock (*see* page 47)
½	cup sweet sherry (cream or amontillado)
½	cup chicken stock or low-sodium canned broth, if needed
2½	tablespoons melted goose fat from the roasting pan
2½	tablespoons all-purpose flour
1	goose liver, cut into small dice
	Salt and ground black pepper

INSTRUCTIONS:

1. Bring reserved goose stock to simmer. Spoon most of fat out of roasting pan, leaving behind all brown roasting particles. Set pan over two burners on low heat. Add sherry; scrape with wooden spoon until all brown glaze in pan is dissolved. Pour mixture into goose stock; simmer to blend flavors, about 5 minutes.

2. Strain mixture into 4-cup glass measure, pressing down on solids with back of spoon; let liquid stand until fat rises to top. Skim fat, and if necessary add enough chicken broth to make up to 2 cups. Rinse out goose stock pot and return strained stock to it. Take gizzard and heart from strainer, cut in tiny dice, and add to goose stock. Return stock to boil.

3. Heat goose fat and flour over medium-low heat in heavy-bottomed medium saucepan, stirring constantly with wooden spoon until roux just begins to color, about 5 minutes; remove from heat. Beating constantly with whisk, pour boiling stock, all at once, into brown roux. Return saucepan to low heat; simmer 3 minutes. Add liver; simmer 1 minute longer. Taste, and adjust seasoning, adding salt and lots of fresh black pepper.

chapter four

ჳ

STUFFED ROAST CORNISH HENS

ORNISH GAME HENS PRESENT SEVERAL CHAL-
lenges to the cook. If roasted breast side up,
the breast will surely overcook before the legs
and thighs are done. Getting the birds to
brown properly with such a short stay in the oven is difficult,
especially if trying to fit six birds into one large pan. And a
500-degree oven is not the answer to any of these problems.
Six little birds dripping fat onto an overheated roasting pan
will set off smoke alarms all over the neighborhood.

Stuffing also presents some challenges. Because the cavity is the last spot to heat up, getting the stuffing to reach a
safe internal temperature of 165 degrees means overcooking

the meat in many cases.

One final problem: After roasting a few batches, we thought the flavor of these birds was unremarkable. Most Cornish hens are mass-produced (companies that specialize in free-range or boutique chickens have not entered this market) and are lacking in flavor. Our mission then was clear—to stuff and roast six grocery-store quality Cornish hens in a way that they looked good (the skin had to brown) and tasted great (we would have to up the flavor in the meat), without overcooking them or smoking up the kitchen.

You may as well steam Cornish hens as roast six of them in a high-sided roasting pan. The pan sides shield the birds from oven heat, and their snug fit in the pan further prevents browning. So our first move was to get the birds up out of the pan and onto a wire rack set over the pan. We also switched to a large roasting pan that measured 19 inches by 13 inches. Our second step was to space the birds as far apart as possible on the rack to insure even cooking and good browning.

From our initial tests, we determined that rotating the birds was crucial for moist, juicy breast meat. Because Cornish hens are in the oven for such a short time, we opted for just one turn as opposed to the two turns we favor when roasting a regular chicken. We found that one turn, from breast side down to breast side up, kept the breast meat from becoming dry or coarse-textured and was not too much of a hassle.

After roasting Cornish hens at temperatures ranging from 350 to 500 degrees, as well as roasting high and finishing low and roasting low and finishing high, we found that all oven temperatures have their problems. We finally settled on 400 degrees, cranking up the oven to 450 degrees during the last few minutes. This roasting temperature was high enough to encourage browning while low enough to prevent excessive smoking. Adding water to the roasting pan once the chicken fat starts to render and the juices flow guarantees a smokeless kitchen. Another perk: The pan is automatically deglazed in the oven. Once the birds are roasted, you can pour the pan juices into a saucepan without having to deglaze the roasting pan over two burners.

Even at these relatively high temperatures, the skin was not quite as brown as we might have liked. We realized that 45 minutes, no matter what the oven temperature, is not enough time to get a dark mahogany skin on any bird. We decided to see if we could improve the appearance of the skin with a glaze of some sort. We tested balsamic vinegar, soy sauce, and jam thinned with a little soy sauce. All three glazes worked beautifully. The balsamic glaze was our favorite, giving the hens a pleasing spotty brown, barbecued look.

With the cooking and skin issues resolved, we turned our attention to boosting the flavor in the bland meat. We doubt that there's a piece of chicken (or turkey) that does not benefit from a few hours in a saltwater brine. Cornish hens are no exception. Two hours in a saltwater bath transformed mediocre-tasting birds into something special.

Our final challenge was to roast the birds, stuffed, without overcooking. Starting the hens breast side down was helping, since it slowed down the cooking in the heat-sensitive breast meat. Heating the stuffing in a microwave before spooning it into each hen also helped. By the time the stuffing reached 165 degrees (a temperature sufficient to kill any salmonella), the breast was 172 degrees and the thigh 176 degrees. As we expected, the thigh was nice and juicy at this temperature. Although we think that breast meat is ideally cooked to 165 to 170 degrees, it was still nice and juicy at this higher temperature and not at all dry, like birds that had been filled with room-temperature stuffing.

Although we were aware that trussing would slow down the roasting of the hens' legs and thighs, we knew we had to do something. With their fragile, loose frame, Cornish hens are unsightly with their dangling legs. Stuffing the birds further increases the need to close the cavity. We discovered that simply tying the legs together improved the look of our hens and secured the stuffing without impeding roasting.

Stuffed Roast Cornish Hens

➤ **NOTE:** *Many game hens in the supermarket weigh more than 1½ pounds, making them too large for a single serving. Try to buy small game hens or go to the butcher and order baby chickens, also called poussin, which generally weigh about one pound.*

Brining the birds breast side down ensures that the meatiest portions are fully submerged. Pouring a little water into the roasting pan at the 25-minute mark, once the birds have been turned, both prevents them from smoking during cooking and makes instant jus, eliminating the need to deglaze the pan over two burners. Each of the stuffing recipes on pages 57–60 yields three cups, enough for six Cornish hens. A quarter-recipe of any bread stuffing in chapter 2 can also be used.

- 2   cups kosher or 1 cup table salt
- 6   Cornish hens (each 1 to 1½ pounds), trimmed of extra fat, giblets removed, rinsed well
- 3   cups prepared stuffing (*see* pages 57–60), heated until very hot (120 to 130 degrees) in microwave
- 6   tablespoons balsamic vinegar
- 3   tablespoons olive oil
- ¼   cup dry vermouth or white wine

⁝⁝ INSTRUCTIONS:

1. Dissolve salt in 5 quarts of cold water in small clean bucket or large bowl. Add hens breast side down; refrigerate 2 to 3 hours. Remove, rinse thoroughly, pat dry, and prick skin all over breast and legs with point of paring knife (*see* figure 17).

2. Adjust oven rack to middle position and heat oven to 400 degrees. Spoon ½ cup of hot stuffing into cavity of each hen; tie legs of each hen together with 10-inch piece of kitchen twine (*see* figure 18). Leaving as much space as possible between each bird, arrange them breast side down and wings facing out, on large (at least 19 by 13 inches) wire rack, set over an equally large roasting or jelly-roll pan. Whisk balsamic vinegar and oil in small bowl; set aside.

3. Roast until backs are golden brown, about 25 minutes. Remove pan from oven, brush bird backs with vinegar and oil glaze (reblending before each bird), turn hens breast side up and wings facing out, and brush breast and leg with additional glaze. Return pan to oven, add 1 cup of water, roast until meat thermometer inserted into stuffed cavity registers about 150 degrees, about 15 to 20 minutes longer. Remove pan from oven again, brush birds with remaining glaze, return pan to oven, add another ½ cup water to pan and increase oven temperature to 450 degrees. Roast until birds are spotty brown and stuffed cavity registers 165 degrees, 5 to 10 minutes. Remove birds from oven and let rest for 10 minutes.

4. Meanwhile, pour hen jus from roasting pan into small saucepan, spoon off excess fat, add vermouth or wine, and simmer over medium-high heat until flavors blend, 2 to 3 minutes. Drizzle about ¼ cup sauce over each hen and serve, passing remaining sauce separately.

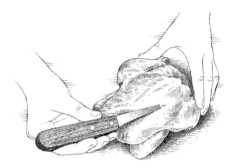

Figure 17.
To prevent skin from ballooning when juices build up, carefully prick the skin (but not the meat) on the breast and legs with the tip of a paring knife before roasting.

Figure 18.
Spoon ½ cup of hot stuffing into the cavity of each hen. Tie the legs of each hen together with a 10-inch piece of kitchen twine.

56

STUFFINGS FOR CORNISH HENS

While any stuffing, including those for turkey (*see* pages 33-37), can be used to fill the cavity in a Cornish hen, the following recipes match beautifully with the delicate flavor of a hen. A Thanksgiving turkey might call for a traditional bread stuffing, but hens can be filled with a variety of grains, including rice, couscous, quinoa, and barley.

Any of these stuffings may be prepared a day in advance, placed in a microwave-safe bowl, wrapped tightly with plastic, and refrigerated. Microwave the stuffing until it is quite hot just before stuffing it into the hens. Each recipe makes enough stuffing for six hens.

Couscous Stuffing with Currants, Apricots, and Pistachios

➤ **NOTE:** *Toasted slivered almonds can be substituted for the pistachio nuts. Makes 3 cups.*

2	tablespoons butter
1	small onion, minced
2	medium garlic cloves, minced
¼	teaspoon ground cinnamon
⅛	teaspoon ground ginger

⅛   teaspoon ground turmeric

1   cup couscous

1⅓   cups chicken stock or low-sodium canned
      chicken broth

¼   cup dried apricots (8 to 9 whole), chopped fine

3   tablespoons currants

¼   cup shelled, toasted pistachio nuts, chopped

2   tablespoons minced fresh parsley leaves

1   teaspoon juice from 1 small lemon
      Salt and ground black pepper

INSTRUCTIONS:

1. Heat butter over medium heat in medium saucepan. Add onion, garlic, cinnamon, ginger, and turmeric; sauté until onion softens, 3 to 4 minutes. Add couscous; stir until well coated, 1 to 2 minutes.

2. Add chicken stock, bring to simmer, remove from heat, cover, and let stand until couscous has fully rehydrated, about 5 minutes. Fluff couscous with fork; stir in dried fruit, nuts, parsley, and lemon juice. Season with salt and pepper to taste. Transfer mixture to microwave-safe bowl.

Wild Rice Stuffing with Cranberries and Toasted Pecans

➤ **NOTE**: *The wild rice blend (a mixture of regular long-grain and wild rice) in this stuffing holds together when pressed with a fork. Look for wild rice blend in the supermarket. You can use all wild rice, but the cooked grains will remain separate. Raisins, currants, or even dried blueberries may be substituted for the cranberries. Makes 3 cups.*

2	cups chicken stock or low-sodium canned chicken broth
1	cup wild rice blend
2	tablespoons butter
1	small onion, minced
½	small celery stalk, minced
¼	cup toasted pecans, chopped coarse
¼	cup dried cranberries
2	tablespoons minced fresh parsley leaves
2	teaspoons minced fresh thyme leaves
	Salt and ground black pepper

⁝⁝ INSTRUCTIONS:

1. Bring chicken stock to boil in medium saucepan. Add rice blend; return to boil. Reduce heat to low, cover, and simmer until rice is fully cooked, 40 to 45 minutes. Turn rice into microwave-safe bowl; fluff with fork.

59

2. Meanwhile, heat butter in medium skillet over medium heat. Add onion and celery; sauté until softened, 3 to 4 minutes. Add this mixture, as well as pecans, cranberries, parsley, and thyme, to rice; toss to coat. Season with salt and pepper to taste.

Quinoa Stuffing with Lemon and Rosemary

➤ **NOTE:** *Quinoa, an ancient South American grain now widely available in supermarkets and natural food stores, grows with a bitter protective coating called saponin that is mostly removed during processing. However, it's still a good idea to rinse quinoa well before cooking. Rich in iron and protein, this grain has a light, crunchy texture and nutty flavor, making it perfect for stuffing small hens. Makes 3 cups.*

1½	cups quinoa, rinsed
3	cups chicken stock or low-sodium canned chicken broth
2	tablespoons butter
1	small onion, chopped fine
1	garlic clove, chopped fine
4	sun-dried tomatoes packed in oil, drained, patted dry, and chopped coarse

1 teaspoon grated zest from 1 lemon
½ teaspoon chopped fresh rosemary leaves
Salt and ground black pepper

INSTRUCTIONS:

1. Combine quinoa and stock in saucepan and bring to boil. Reduce heat to low and simmer until liquid is absorbed, 10 to 15 minutes. Transfer to microwave-safe bowl.

2. Meanwhile melt butter in small skillet over medium heat. Add onion and garlic; sauté until softened, 3 to 4 minutes. Add this mixture, along with sun-dried tomatoes, zest, rosemary, and salt and pepper to taste, to quinoa; toss to coat.

chapter five

ᘔ

BAKED HAM

H AM IS MADE FROM THE HIND QUARTER OF a hog. There are two general categories, which are referred to by butchers and people in the business as country and city hams. Country hams are salted and aged by a process known as dry-curing. City hams are brined in a salt solution (like pickles) by a process known as wet-curing. The former method results in salty, firm, dry meat, like prosciutto or the famed serrano ham of Spain. The latter process is used to make moister slicing hams, the kind sold in supermarkets.

Most country hams are made in small batches by craftsmen on farms in Virginia, the Carolinas, Kentucky, and

Tennessee. Unless you live in the South, you won't see country hams in markets, but they can be ordered by mail or through your local butcher.

Country hams are cured in salt or a mixture of salt and sugar for several weeks, usually about five. During this dry-curing period, the meat must lose at least 18 percent of its fresh weight. (Many country hams shed 25 percent of their weight, for an even saltier, more concentrated ham flavor.) By law, a country ham must also absorb at least 4 percent salt. At this level, the salt acts as preservative and prevents any bacterial growth during the long aging process that follows.

Once a country ham has been cured, it's smoked (over hardwoods like hickory or apple) for two to six days, rubbed with black pepper, and then aged, at least 60 days and up to a year or more in some cases. You could eat country ham raw (it's fully preserved), but the custom in the United States is to cook ham. The most famous country hams come from the small Virginia town of Smithfield. By law, Smithfield hams must be dry-cured and then aged a minimum of six months.

The flavor of a country ham is always intense, and often quite salty. Good country ham has a complex smoky flavor with hints of blue cheese, nuts, wood, and spice. In general, the longer a ham has been aged, the stronger the flavors will be. When buying country ham, decide how strong and intense a flavor you like and then buy according to age. Most novices will find a 15-month ham overpowering and are probably better off with a shorter-cure ham. Southerners who grew up on good country ham may find a three-month ham insipid.

Many people believe that soaking a country ham is essential to its final edibility. The theory is that soaking causes the meat to lose some of the salt with which it was cured, as the salt naturally moves from places of greater concentration (in the ham) to places of lesser concentration (the soaking water). As salt migrates out of the ham, water replaces some of it, a process that helps soften the ham's texture and prevents excessive dryness.

Our testing supported this theory but also showed that the process doesn't happen as quickly as you might think. Only when we soaked a year-old ham for a full 36 hours could we detect any change in texture compared with a similar ham that was not soaked. The soaked ham was just a bit less dry and a bit less salty.

In our tests, we found that hams subjected to cures of less than six months are rarely so salty that they need soaking. But a ham cured for more than a year needs at least three days in cold water before cooking to become edible. Hams cured for six to 12 months need to be soaked for 36 hours.

Many recipes suggest adding ingredients, especially

sweeteners, to the soaking liquid. We found that sugar, Coke, and white vinegar (all recommended by various sources) have no effect on the ham.

The next step is to cook the ham. We tried baking the ham in a 325-degree oven and liked the results quite a lot. The ham is dry and salty. However, this method is for ham lovers only. Many ham novices were put off by the strong flavor. Simmering tames some of the salt and is the best bet when preparing ham for a holiday crowd. Simmering also adds a little moisture to the ham, making it easier to carve in thin slices. (Country ham is too rich and salty to be sliced into thick slabs like a city ham.)

We tried all kinds of simmering regimens and found that cooking the ham at the barest simmer is better than boiling. Gentle heat ensures that the outside layers of meat don't cook too fast. As for the timing, we found that 10 minutes per pound is a decent barometer. Better still, use an instant-read thermometer and pull the ham out of the pot when it reaches 120 degrees.

At this point, the rind and most of the fat need to be removed. The ham can then be scored, glazed, and put into the oven just to set the glaze, the best option when serving the ham as the centerpiece of a meal. A simmered country ham can also be cooled, boned, weighted, and then sliced into very thin pieces and served at a buffet party with biscuits.

Many cooks would rather skip the scrubbing, soaking, and simmering steps that a country ham often requires. They would also prefer a ham that could be carved into thick, moist slices. Wet-cured city hams are the answer. City hams are smoked like country hams but not aged. Unlike country hams, brined hams are not actually preserved and must be refrigerated like fresh meat.

There are several types of city hams. Some hams are labeled "boneless," others "bone-in." Boneless hams are usually made by pressing together various pieces of meat. There is no muscle definition and the "skin" is often made by a machine that scores the exterior and then paints it with food coloring. We prefer bone-in city hams. The large hip bone that runs the length of the ham has been left intact. However, some or all of the small bones that can make carving a country ham so tricky have been removed.

The other issue is the water content. Many large commercial outfits inject the meat with brine to increase its weight and cost (hams are usually sold by the pound), sometimes by as much as 25 percent. Hams that are actually brined instead of injected taste stronger and are more economical since you are not paying for water weight that the ham will lose when cooked. If you see the words "with natural juices" or "water added," the ham has been injected and will probably cook up moister, less smoky, and much lighter. If you want a really mild ham flavor, you might consider a water-added ham. However, our recommendation is to stick with a no-water-added ham. They are chewy rather than squishy and have some of the character of a country ham without all the bother and the salt.

Some city hams are sold with a partial rind and some fat that must be trimmed, just like a country ham. However, most city hams have very little fat and cannot even be scored. If you have a choice, buy a ham with some fat on it. You can then remove as much fat as you like and score whatever remains.

To serve a city ham, simply glaze and bake. We recommend buying a city ham that is labeled "ready-to-eat" or "fully cooked." (Most city hams are sold this way.) If fully cooked at the plant, you need only warm the ham in the oven to an internal temperature of 140 degrees. If you happen to buy a ham labeled "partially cooked" or "cook before eating," it must baked to an internal temperature of 160 degrees, and you will need to adjust the cooking times in our recipe.

Baked Country Ham

➤ **NOTE:** *We tested nine brands of mail-order country hams. All but one of the hams was deemed good or excellent. We particularly liked the Wigwam ham from S. Wallace Edwards & Sons (800-222-4267).*

Any size dry-cured ham can be adapted to this recipe; just adjust the cooking time as needed to reach the internal temperatures listed below. Country ham is best served in very thin slices over biscuits or in rolls. It's much too rich and salty to serve in thick slices. Leftover bits of ham can be used to flavor cooked greens, eggs, pasta, or rice. If removing the hock, save it to flavor soup or beans. Serves about 30.

1   **country ham, 14 to 15 pounds**
1   **cup glaze of choice (*see* pages 74 and 75)**

▪ **INSTRUCTIONS:**

1. Scrub mold off (*see* figure 19). Remove hock with hacksaw (*see* figure 20). If ham has been aged less than six months, proceed with step 2. If ham has been aged more than six months, place ham in large stock pot filled with cool water. Place pot in cool place and change water once a day. Hams aged 6 to 12 months should be soaked for 36 hours. Hams aged more than a year should be soaked for 3 days. Drain ham and scrub again.

2. Place ham in large stock pot and cover with fresh water.

Bring to boil, reduce heat, and simmer until instant-read thermometer inserted into thickest part of ham registers 120 degrees, 2 to 3 hours. Transfer ham from pot to large cutting board. (Liquid can be reserved and used to cook greens or rice, or added to soup.)

3. Preheat oven to 325 degrees. When ham has cooled just enough to handle, peel away rind and most of fat (*see* figures 21 and 22). Score remaining fat (*see* figure 23).

4. Place ham on flat rack in large roasting pan lined with double layer of aluminum foil. Pour 2 cups water into pan. Smear glaze onto exterior of ham using rubber spatula (*see* figure 24). Bake until instant-read thermometer inserted in several places in ham registers 140 degrees, about 1 hour. Transfer ham to cutting board and let rest about 15 minutes. Carve into very thin slices and serve.

Figure 19.
Scrub mold off with a vegetable scrubbing brush under running
water. Hams aged more than six months should be soaked. Scrub
ham again after soaking.

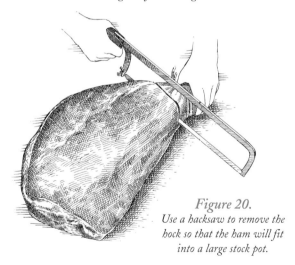

Figure 20.
Use a hacksaw to remove the
hock so that the ham will fit
into a large stock pot.

Figure 21.
As soon as the ham is removed from the simmering water,
remove the skin and most, but not all, of the fat. Slice into the
rind with a sharp knife.

Figure 22.
Peel back the rind and discard. With knife, trim remaining fat to
about ¼ inch thickness.

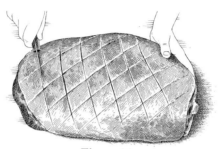

Figure 23.

Country hams as well as any city hams that have an even outer
layer of fat should be scored before baking. Use a sharp paring
knife to cut down into the fat, making sure not to cut into the
meat. Cut parallel lines across the ham, spacing them about 1½
inches apart. Make a series of perpendicular lines to create a
diamond pattern in the fat.

Figure 24.

Use a rubber spatula to apply the thick, paste-like glaze to the
exterior of the partially cooked ham.

72

Baked City Ham

➤ **N O T E :** *A whole brined or wet-cured ham can weigh as much as 16 pounds. However, many companies sell portions of the leg, which can weigh as little as five pounds. Cook the ham according to internal temperature rather than time, and use more or less glaze depending on size of ham. Serves six to 20, depending on size of ham.*

>**1**   **wet-cured, fully cooked bone-in ham**
>   **(5 to 16 pounds)**
>**½–1**   **cup glaze of choice (*see* pages 74 and 75)**

▚ **I N S T R U C T I O N S :**

1. Let ham sit at room temperature for at least 3 hours. Adjust oven rack to lowest position. Heat oven to 325 degrees.

2. Remove wrapping. If ham is covered with jelly-like layer, rinse and pat dry. If necessary, remove rind and trim fat to ¼-inch thickness (*see* figure 22). If covered with even layer of fat, score ham (*see* figure 23).

3. Place ham on flat rack in large roasting pan lined with double layer of aluminum foil. Pour 2 cups water into pan. Bake ham until instant-read thermometer inserted in several places in ham registers 120 degrees, 1 to 3 hours, depending on size of ham. Smear glaze onto exterior of ham using rubber spatula (*see* figure 24). Continue baking until instant-read thermometer registers 140 degrees, about 1 hour longer. Let ham rest for about 15 minutes. Carve perpendicular to bone into ½-inch-thick slices.

Orange Juice and Brown Sugar Glaze

➤ **NOTE**: *For a sweeter, glossier glaze, brush ham with a little honey about 30 minutes before it is ready to come out of the oven. We don't like to chew on whole cloves so we don't stud the ham; we prefer adding the flavor of cloves to the glaze. Don't baste the ham with any of the pan juices. They are too salty and intense. Makes about 1 cup.*

1 ¼	cups packed light brown sugar
3	tablespoons fresh squeezed orange juice
½	teaspoon ground cloves

INSTRUCTIONS:

Mix sugar, orange juice, and cloves together in medium bowl to form thick paste. Set mixture aside until ready to glaze ham.

Mustard and Brown Sugar Glaze

➤ **NOTE:** *For a sweeter, glossier glaze, brush ham with a little maple syrup about 30 minutes before it is ready to come out of the oven. Makes about 1 cup.*

1¼	cups packed light brown sugar
¼	cup Dijon mustard
½	teaspoon ground cloves

INSTRUCTIONS:

Mix sugar, mustard, and cloves together in medium bowl to form thick paste. Set mixture aside until ready to glaze ham.

chapter six

PRIME RIB

E STARTED OUR TESTING WITH OVEN temperatures. We tested eight heating regimens, everything from 500 degrees for 40 minutes with the oven turned off and the door closed for the next two hours to a constant 200 degrees. All the prime ribs roasted at 300 degrees or above were pretty much the same. Each slice of carved beef was well done around the exterior and medium towards the center, with a beautiful medium-rare pink center. We might have been tempted to report that roasting temperature doesn't matter if we hadn't tried cooking prime rib at lower temperatures.

It's funny that we should end up preferring the prime rib roasted at 200 degrees because it certainly wasn't love at first sight. About halfway through this roast's cooking time, the meat looked virtually raw and the exterior was pale. But we changed our minds quickly as soon as we carved the first slice. This roast was as beautiful on the inside as it was anemic on the outside. Unlike the roasts cooked at higher temperatures, this one was rosy pink from the surface to the center. If was also the juiciest and most tender roast we had cooked. It was restaurant prime rib at its best.

Besides being evenly cooked, the prime rib roasted in a 200-degree oven had another thing going for it: Its internal temperatures increased only a degree or two during its resting period. (Roasts are allowed to rest when they come out of the oven both to distribute the heat evenly and to allow the juices to reabsorb back into the outer layer of meat.) Cooked to 128 degrees, it moved only to 130 degrees after a 45-minute rest.

Not so the roasts cooked at higher temperatures. Their internal temperatures increased much more dramatically out of the oven. As a matter of fact, we noticed a direct correlation between oven temperature and a roast's post-cooking temperature increase. Roasts cooked in a moderate oven (325 to 350 degrees) averaged a 14-degree jump in internal temperature while resting. Roasts cooked at 425 degrees jumped an unbelievable 24 degrees on the counter. These temperature rises make it difficult to know when a roast should be taken out of the oven.

In addition to its more stable internal temperature, the prime rib roasted at 200 degrees also lost less weight during cooking than those roasted at higher temperatures. Roasts weighing about seven pounds shed less than eight ounces when cooked at 200 degrees, but almost 1½ pounds in a 350-degree oven and a shocking two pounds at 425 degrees. Some of the weight loss may be extra fat, but some is surely juice. This test confirmed our sense that beef roasted at 200 degrees was indeed the juiciest.

The Beef Council and other official agencies won't endorse low-temperature roasting. But after conversations with several food scientists, we determined that low-temperature roasting is safe for this cut. The odds of finding bacteria inside a prime rib roast are virtually nonexistent. (Bacteria in beef is usually limited to the exterior or to ground beef.) Just as important, the only way to guarantee that all bacteria are killed is to cook the meat to an internal temperature of 160 degrees, something we would never suggest. The only possible problem is bacteria on the exterior of the meat.

But we took care of this problem (as well as the pale exterior of the roast cooked at 200 degrees) when we decided to sear the meat on top of the stove before putting it in the oven. To make sure that the final color is attractive, sear the roast for at least eight minutes, turning it often.

Our last area of interest was aging. From past tests, we knew that dry-aging often improves the flavor and texture of steaks. However, most butchers don't dry-age beef because the hanging quarters take up too much refrigerator space and the meat loses weight during the process, forcing the butcher to make less profit or raise the price of the beef. Most butchers prefer beef that comes packaged in vacuum-sealed bags. There is no work and no weight loss.

We were still curious about dry-aging, so we ordered two prime ribs, one dry-aged, one wet-aged, from a restaurant supplier in Manhattan. Like a good, young red wine, the wet-aged beef tasted pleasant and fresh on its own. But there was no comparison to the dry-aged beef, which had a stronger, richer, gamier flavor and buttery texture.

Since dry-aged beef is so hard to find, we set out to devise our own method. It's just a matter of making room in the refrigerator and remembering to buy the roast ahead of time. Simply pat the roast dry and place it on a rack over a pan. We found that even a day or two helped concentrate the meat's flavor. For an especially tender texture and beefy flavor, let the meat age for the full week.

Perfect Prime Rib

➤ **NOTE:** *Even if you don't purchase the roast several days ahead of time as the instructions suggest, even a day or two of aging in the refrigerator will help. The roast is first browned on top of the stove and then placed in the oven. You can accomplish both steps in a heavy-duty roasting pan. Otherwise, brown the roast in a cast-iron skillet and then transfer it to a regular roasting pan. It is essential that the temperature inside your oven is actually 200 degrees. Some ovens can run a bit cool at such low settings. Use an oven thermometer and, if necessary, boost the thermostat as needed to maintain a constant temperature of 200 degrees inside the oven. Serves six to eight.*

> 1   3-rib standing rib roast (about 7 pounds),
> preferably first cut (*see* figure 25)
> Salt and ground black pepper

⠿ INSTRUCTIONS:

1. Set roast on rack above pan lined with paper towels. Refrigerate for 3 to 7 days. Shave off dehydrated exterior layer of roast with sharp knife. Let roast rest at room temperature for 3 hours; tie roast (*see* figure 26).

2. Adjust oven rack to low position and heat oven to 200 degrees. Heat large heavy-duty roasting pan over two burners set at medium heat. Place roast in hot pan and cook on all sides until nicely browned and at least ¼ cup fat has rendered, 8 to 10 minutes. Remove roast from pan. Drain off fat.

80

(Reserve fat in measuring cup if making Yorkshire pudding.) Set wide rack in pan, then set roast on rack. Generously season with salt and pepper.

3. Place roast in oven and roast until meat registers 130 degrees (for medium-rare), about 3½ hours (or about 30 minutes per pound). Transfer prime rib to cutting board. (If making Yorkshire pudding, *see* recipe on page 83.) Let roast stand 20 minutes (a bit longer is fine) before serving.

4. Remove twine and position roast so that rib bones are perpendicular to cutting board. Using carving fork to hold roast in place, cut along rib bones to sever meat from bones. Set roast cut side down on board and carve meat across grain into thick slices.

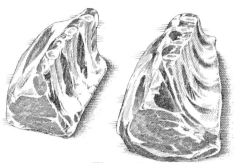

Figure 25.

*Butchers tend to cut a rib roast, which consists of ribs six through
12, into two distinct cuts. We find that the loin end rib roast (left),
also called the "first cut" or "small end" roast, is more tender and less
fatty because it contains a single rib-eye muscle. This roast, consist-
ing of ribs ten through 12, is our favorite. The "second cut" rib roast
(right) includes ribs six through nine. It is closer to the chuck end
and consists of several muscles, each of which is surrounded by fat.*

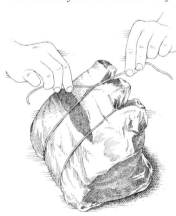

Figure 26.
*It is imperative to tie
prime rib before roasting.
If left untied, the outer
layer of meat will pull
away from the rib-eye
muscle and overcook. To
prevent this problem, tie
the roast at both ends,
running string parallel to
the bone.*

Yorkshire Pudding

➤ **NOTE:** *Many recipes insist that the batter for Yorkshire pudding must be cold to rise properly. We found that the batter will rise fine whether it goes into the oven at room temperature or well chilled. The temperature of the pan does matter, though. If the pan is not hot, the pudding will be flat and soggy. We suggest using the fat rendered during the searing process. Or, if you prefer, melt butter in the empty pan. Make sure to cook Yorkshire pudding fully or it might fall. It should be well puffed and nicely browned. Serves six to eight.*

- 2 **cups all-purpose flour**
- 1 **teaspoon salt**
- 2 **cups milk**
- 5 **large eggs**
- ¼ **cup rendered beef fat or butter**

INSTRUCTIONS:

1. Whisk flour and salt together in large bowl. Beat milk and eggs together in medium bowl until well combined. Slowly whisk wet ingredients into dry ingredients until batter is smooth. There should be no lumps of flour.

2. When roast is removed from oven, raise temperature to 425 degrees. Pour fat into 9- by 13-inch pan and heat in oven for about 10 minutes.

3. Whisk batter to recombine. Pour batter into hot pan. Bake until puffed and nicely browned, about 25 minutes. Cut into squares and serve immediately with prime rib.

chapter seven

ROAST LEG
OF LAMB

THE MAIN PROBLEM WITH ROAST LEG OF lamb is that it cooks unevenly. In most cases, the outer meat becomes dry and gray, while the meat around the bone remains almost raw. Since the leg is reasonably priced and feeds a lot of people, it seemed worth solving this basic cooking problem.

The uneven thickness of the leg is the most formidable obstacle to even cooking. At the thicker sirloin end, the meat surrounding the flat, twisting hipbone is very thin. The center of the leg, which comprises the top half of the thigh, is fleshy, but the thigh then tapers dramatically toward the knee joint, and the shank itself is a mere nub of meat.

The only way to deal with the problem is to remove the hipbone entirely and then tie the leg into as compact a shape as possible. However, boning and tying do not by themselves guarantee even cooking. Special procedures must be followed in roasting the leg to ensure that all parts are exposed to the same amount of heat and will thus reach similar internal temperatures at the same time.

We started by roasting a 7½-pound leg at 400 degrees, with the meat resting directly on the roasting pan. After about one hour, the meaty side of the leg, which had been facing up, registered 120 on a meat thermometer, or underdone. The meat around the thigh bone was practically raw, while the bottom of the leg, which had been resting on the hot pan, had reached 135 degrees, or slightly overdone.

Clearly we needed a rack to protect the downward-facing side of the leg from overcooking. We also felt the exterior could be browner and that a lower cooking temperature might even out the rate at which various parts of the leg cook. We roasted a leg on a rack at 450 degrees for 20 minutes and then lowered the temperature to 325 degrees for the next hour. The top was evenly cooked, at 130 degrees throughout, but the underside was undercooked. Evidently, the rack had been too effective in keeping the bottom of the leg cool.

We decided to try the next leg with the oven rack at the

lowest position, so that the rack side of the leg might cook more quickly. This helped, but we decided in the end that the leg would have to be turned for even cooking.

We had one final question: Was it worth trying to find Prime rather than the standard Choice lamb. Tasting them side-by-side, we preferred the Prime cut, which was more tender. The Choice leg was a bit chewy, while the Prime leg was silky and buttery. The flavor of the Prime leg was also less gamy and richer, almost like roast beef. The differences, especially in texture, were most apparent in slices taken from the rarest portion of the roasts. So if you like rare lamb, it's definitely worth ordering a Prime leg. It only costs an extra 50 cents or so a pound, but you will have to find a butcher shop that carries this sometimes hard-to-find meat.

Roast Leg of Lamb

➤ **NOTE:** *There are two choices when shopping for leg of lamb. A whole leg contains all the bones. Many markets sell "semiboneless" legs, which have the aitchbone, or hipbone, removed (see figure 27). The lamb cooks more evenly (and makes carving much simpler) when the aitchbone is removed, so ask your butcher to do this if necessary. If making the Piquant Caper Sauce, you will need the aitchbone to make stock. Ask the butcher to wrap it up separately. Many legs also come with a "hinged" shank bone. Unless you have a very large roasting pan, you will need to remove this part of the shank bone to fit the roast in the oven (see figure 27). This bone can also be used to make stock in the Piquant Caper Sauce.*

Legs come in a variety of sizes. Our recipe starts with a semiboneless leg that weighs between six and eight pounds. (The weight of the whole, untrimmed leg is about 1½ pounds more.) Smaller legs have a sweeter, milder flavor, so you may want to search for a petite leg if you don't like a strong "sheepy" flavor. If roasting a smaller leg, reduce the cooking time at 325 degrees by at least 10 minutes.

We find it best to cook lamb by internal temperature. We like our lamb medium-rare, or about 135 degrees when carved. Since the internal temperature will rise while the lamb rests, pull the leg out of the oven when the temperature reaches 130 degrees. If you like lamb on the rarer side, pull it out of the oven at 120 degrees (the temperature will rise to 125 degrees by carving time). If you like lamb more well done, pull it out at 135 degrees (the temperature will rise above 140 degrees). Depending on the size of the leg you buy, this recipe serves eight to 12.

Roast Leg of Lamb

Salt and ground black pepper

1 teaspoon finely minced fresh rosemary leaves or
½ teaspoon dried rosemary, finely crushed
(omit if making Mint Sauce on page 95)

1 semiboneless leg of lamb (6 to 8 pounds), excess
fat removed and discarded (*see* figures 28–31)

3 medium garlic cloves, slivered

2 tablespoons olive oil

■ INSTRUCTIONS:

1. Mix 2 teaspoons salt, 2 teaspoons pepper, and rosemary
in small bowl.

2. Sprinkle portion of rosemary mixture over inner surface
of cleaned and boned meat. Tie lamb according to figures
32 and 33. Cut slits into roast with tip of paring knife. Poke
garlic slivers inside. Brush exterior with oil, then rub
remaining seasoning onto all surfaces of meat. Place leg,
meaty side up, on roasting pan fitted with flat rack; let stand
30 minutes. Adjust oven rack to lowest position and heat
oven to 450 degrees.

3. Pour ½ cup water into bottom of roasting pan. Roast lamb
for 10 minutes. With wad of paper toweling in each hand,
turn leg over. Roast 10 minutes longer. Lower oven temperature to 325 degrees. Turn leg meaty side up and continue

88

roasting, turning leg every 20 minutes, until instant-read thermometer inserted in several locations registers 130 degrees, 60 to 80 minutes longer. Transfer roast to another pan; cover with foil and set aside in warm spot to complete cooking and to allow juices to reabsorb into meat, 15 to 20 minutes. Reserve roasting pan to make Piquant Caper Sauce.

4. When ready to serve, remove string from roast and carve by cutting slices parallel to bone, each about ¼-inch thick. When meat on top has been removed, flip leg over and carve bottom in same fashion. To facilitate carving side of leg, grasp narrow end of leg and hold it perpendicular to work surface and slice as before. Serve sliced lamb with sauce.

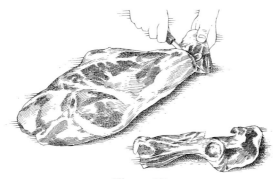

Figure 27.
The butcher should remove the aitchbone (right front) and save it so you can make stock. If the shank bone has been partially detached by the butcher, remove it with a knife and save it, too, for stock.

89

Figure 28.

Lamb fat is strong-flavored and unpleasant to chew. Remove
large pieces of fat, using a knife and your hands to cut and then
pull the fat off the leg. It's fine to leave a few streaks of fat to
moisten the roast.

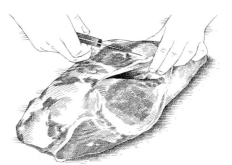

Figure 29.

The fat and other material surrounding the strong-tasting
popliteal lymph node should be removed. Set the leg meaty side up
and cut down into the area that separates the broad, thin flap of
meat on one side of the leg with the thick, meaty lobe on the other.

Figure 30.
Use both hands and the knife to widen the incision, exposing the lymph node and surrounding fat.

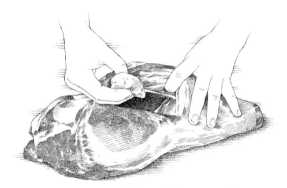

Figure 31.
Reach in and grasp the nugget of fat. Pull while cutting the connective tissue, being very careful not to cut into the gland itself. Pull the fat and other matter free.

91

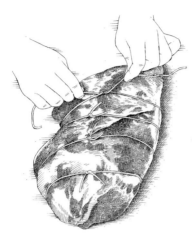

Figure 32.
Set the leg meaty side up and smooth the flap of meat at the sirloin end so that it folds over and neatly covers the tip of the thigh bone. Tie several short lengths of twine around the leg, placing each piece of twine parallel to the next.

Figure 33.
Tie several more short lengths of twine around the leg, running pieces of twine perpendicular to those in figure 32.

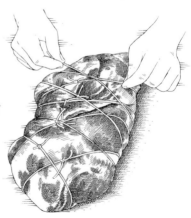

Piquant Caper Sauce

➤ NOTE: *If making this sauce, ask the butcher for the aitchbone (see figure 27) and reserve any meat scraps that have come off the lamb during the cleaning process. Make sure to remove the fat from these scraps. You can also use the hinged part of the shank bone (see figure 27). To accommodate the aitchbone, you will need a wide saucepan or deep sauté pan. Start the sauce as soon as the lamb goes into the oven.*

1	tablespoon olive oil
	Lamb bones and meat scraps
1	medium onion, chopped coarse
3	cups chicken stock or canned chicken broth, preferably low-sodium
⅓	cup dry white wine or dry vermouth
2	tablespoons unsalted butter, softened
2	tablespoons all-purpose flour
⅓	cup (3 ounces) small capers, drained, bottling liquid reserved
1	teaspoon balsamic vinegar

■■ INSTRUCTIONS:

1. Heat oil in large, heavy-bottomed saucepan set over medium heat. Add reserved bones and meat scraps and onion. Sauté, turning bones several times, until well browned, about 10 minutes. Add broth, scraping pan bottom to loosen browned bits; bring to boil. Reduce heat to low; simmer, partially covered, until bones and meat have given up their flavor to broth, about 1 hour. Add a little water if bones are more than half exposed during cooking.

2. Set empty pan used to roast leg of lamb over medium heat. Add wine and scrape with wooden spoon until brown bits dissolve. Pour mixture into lamb stock, then strain everything into 2-cup glass measure. Let sit until fat rises, then skim. Add water, if necessary, to make 1½ cups of liquid. Pour liquid back into saucepan and bring to boil.

3. Mix butter and flour to smooth paste. Gradually whisk butter-flour mixture into stock. Stir in capers, vinegar, and any juices lamb throws off while resting. Simmer to blend flavors, about 3 minutes. Add more vinegar or caper bottling liquid to achieve piquant, subtly sharp-sweet sauce. Serve with lamb.

Mint Sauce

➤ **NOTE:** *This sauce has a refreshing mint flavor without the cloying sweetness of mint jelly. The texture is much thinner than jelly, similar to maple syrup. This sauce is remarkably easy to make and does not require any bones since no stock is necessary. If making this sauce, eliminate the rosemary from the lamb recipe and just rub the meat with olive oil and salt and pepper and stud with garlic. Chop the mint right before adding it to the sauce to preserve its fresh flavor.*

    1   **cup white wine vinegar**
    6   **tablespoons sugar**
  ¼   **cup minced fresh mint leaves**

⠿ **INSTRUCTIONS:**

1. Heat vinegar and sugar in medium saucepan over medium heat. Bring to boil and simmer until slightly syrupy, 8 to 10 minutes. (Liquid should be reduced to about ½ cup.)

2. Remove pan from heat, let cool for 5 minutes, and stir in mint. Pour sauce into bowl and cover with plastic wrap. Set aside for at least 1 hour. (Sauce can be set aside for one day.) Serve at room temperature with lamb.

index